The Embroiderer's Book of Designs

The Embroiderer's Book of Designs

LEE LOCKHEED

PUBLICATIONS

Distributed By
Quilters' Resource Inc.
Chicago, IL 60614
1-312 278-5695

First published 1994

Written & Illustrated by Lee Lockheed

Publisher: *Tracy Marsh*
Photographer: *Adam Bruzzone*
Photographic Stylist: *Lee Lockheed*
Editor: *Susan Gray*
Designer: *Peta Nugent*

National Library of Australia
Cataloguing-in-publication data.

Lockheed, Lee.
The embroiderer's Book of designs.

ISBN 1 86438 800 5
1. Embroidery - Patterns I. Title
746.44041

Published by
TRACY MARSH PUBLICATIONS PTY LTD
PO Box 643
Strawberry Hills
N.S.W. Australia, 2012
Telephone: (02) 318 0488 Fax: (02)319 3731

Printed and bound in Hong Kong

Dedication

To Sarah and Amy

Acknowledgements

I would like to thank Richard, my husband, and my daughters Sarah and Amy for their love and support. Thanks to Richard for transcribing my handwritten manuscript into the typed word.

***To the following individuals and companies
I would like to offer my sincere thanks for
their encouragement and assistance:***

Myer Adelaide, South Australia, for donations of fabric
and the loan of items used for photography.
Joyce Nicholson for organising embroidery
classes in the Myer City Store, South Australia.
All of my students, and shop owners throughout
Australia for their continuing support.
Ann and Russ Balmer of Tea Tree
Gallery and Framing, South Australia.
Diana de Hauteclocque and Jennifer Britton
of Stadia Handcrafts, New South Wales.
Margaret and Bill Mansell, Persian
Cat Breeders of South Australia.
Cate Grundy for the Elephant Pattern on page 21
and for allowing me to use her
embroidered Silk Rabbit on page 30.
Valerie Kidd, Judy Coombe, Eulie Henderson,
Pam Whitehouse, Libby Stubbs, Janine Swayne and
Melissa Pollard for the loan of items used for photography.
Jane Smith for constructing the cushion cover on
page 16 and for binding the Bluebird Blanket on page 78.
Carrie Schultz, cake decorator extrordinaire.

Contents

INTRODUCTION
Page 8

GENERAL INFORMATION

EMBROIDERY DESIGNS

GLOSSARY OF STITCHES

Introduction

Due to the overwhelming response to my first book,
Wool Embroidery and Design, and from my teaching trips throughout Australia,
I discovered that there was a real need for new and exciting embroidery
designs. In the hope of renewing enthusiasm for the artistic scope of this
medium, I set about creating a set of embroidery designs which
I felt would complement the collection from the first book.

The new designs presented here range from the tiny, delicate roses of the
Lavender Bag through to the field of flowers of the Summer Garland.
Embroidery is one of the most satisfying ways of embellishing fabric items, from
rugs, cushions, boxes, basket lids, potpourri bags and toys, transforming them
into unique treasures. This book contains twenty-five detailed designs in cotton,
wool and silk, all accompanied by full colour photographs. Helpful keys show
the stitches and threads used in each design, while every stitch used in the book
is included in the Glossary of Stitches. The superb photographs and designs in
this book will provide you not only with a visual opportunity to simply enjoy,
but also with the inspiration to pick up a needle and create.

Lee Lockheed

Materials

THREADS

For the projects featured in this book, the following threads have been chosen. All are readily available through most specialist embroidery outlets.

♦ DMC Tapestry Wools *(Art No. 486)*, lightly twisted 4 ply
♦ DMC Broder Medicis *(Art No. 475)*, 2 ply crewel wool
♦ DMC Stranded Cotton *(Art No. 117)*, 100% cotton lustrous thread in six separable strands - use one strand only
♦ Rajmahal *(Art silk/viscose)*, a thread with a shiny finish in six separable strands
♦ Silk Ribbon, 100% silk
♦ Gold and silver metallic thread
♦ Tubular Knitting Ribbon

ACCESSORIES

♦ Mill Hill Glass Beads
♦ Metal cupids
♦ Dough roses
♦ Dough fairies

The dough roses and fairies can be replaced with embroidered flowers if preferred. *(See Fairy Garland on page 48)*

NEEDLES

♦ DMC Tapestry Wool - Size 18 Tapestry
♦ DMC Broder Medicis, DMC Stranded Cotton and Rajmahal Thread - Size 5/10 Embroidery Crewel
♦ Silk Ribbon - Size 24 or 26 Chenille or Tapestry

PENS

♦ Hot Iron Transfer Pencil *(see Transferring Designs)*
♦ Birch Marking Pen with Eraser - purple water-soluble ink on one end and white eraser ink on the other end. This pen is excellent for drawing pattens or marking designs on all types of fabric.

Transferring Designs

HOT IRON TRANSFER PENCIL

A transfer pencil can be used successfully on such fabrics as linen, cotton, calico and silk. Draw the pattern on heavy-duty tracing paper, turn the paper over and trace over the lines with the transfer pencil. Pin or tack the design (transfer pencil side down) onto the fabric. Run a hot iron over the transfer for a few seconds. Carefully lift a corner of the paper to make sure that the design is transferring. The Bluebird Blanket on page 79 has been transferred in this manner. Extreme care must be taken, however, not to scorch the wool.

TRANSFERRING DESIGNS ONTO WOOL

Trace the design onto good quality tracing paper. Tack or pin the design onto the woollen fabric and, with a sharp lead pencil or water-soluble fabric pen, pierce a hole through the centre of each design element and mark a small dot on the fabric. When you remove the tracing paper you are left with the dots that locate the centre of each flower on which you can now work the design. If embroidering a large design, break it into smaller, more workable sections.

TRANSFERRING BOWS

To transfer a bow, cut out the template of paper and tack it to the fabric. Using the same colour thread as the bow, outline the shape using a small tacking stitch. Unpick the tacking holding the template to the fabric and remove the paper. Satin stitch the bow, working either side of the tacking stitches.

Making up Projects

The aim of this book is to provide twenty-five new embroidery designs, each of them adaptable to a range of projects limited only by one's imagination. For this reason, *The Embroiderer's Book of Designs* is not a book of projects but a collection of original designs. The photographs depict one interpretation of each, while the lists of project ideas under each embroidery heading offer inspiration for other ways of applying the design. Outlined below are brief instructions for how to construct those designs which have a pattern included.

All pattern pieces include a 5 mm seam allowance.

TEDDY BEARS

Embroider the design onto fabric. Cut two pattern pieces. With right sides together, stitch around the bear, leaving a small opening on the outer side of one leg. Turn right side out, stuff with toy filler and slip stitch the opening. Once padded, sew along the stitching line shown on the pattern pieces to give shape to the bear's ears and arms.

LAVENDER BAG

The shoe filler pattern is also used for the lavender bag. Embroider the design onto silk or organdie. Cut two pattern pieces. With right sides facing, sew the pattern pieces together. Turn right side out and turn over a 5 mm seam. Turn over another seam 3 cm wide and stem stitch right around. Fill with lavender and roses and tie with a bow.

SILK RIBBON ELEPHANT & BABY ELEPHANT

Embroider the design onto silk fabric. Cut two pattern pieces. With right sides together, stitch around the elephant, leaving a small opening. Turn the pattern pieces right side out, fill with toy filler and slip stitch the opening. The elephant's tail is plaited using six pieces of Rajmahal thread no. 226 *(grey)*.

SHOE FILLERS

Embroider the design onto the fabric. Cut two pattern pieces, or four if you wish to line the shoe fillers. With right sides facing, sew the pattern pieces together. Fill with toy filler, pot pourri, or a mixture of both, and tie with a silk ribbon bow.

SILK RABBIT

Embroider the design onto silk. Cut two pattern pieces. With right sides together, stitch around the rabbit, leaving a small opening. Turn right side out, stuff with toy filler and slip stitch the opening. Stem stitch the outline of the rabbit and attach a small piece of acrylic fur for the tail.

Silk Ribbon Basket

A basket of spring flowers lends a sunny touch to a room, and this design, embroidered using silk ribbons, will bring pleasure to both its maker and to those who look upon it.

PROJECT IDEAS

Pocket Design
Child's Collar
Brush & Mirror Set
Jewellery Cushion
Covered Box
Lingerie Bag

Silk Ribbon Basket

Forget-Me-Nots
Colonial Knot Centre

Silk Ribbon 2 mm 124, 126 *(blues)*
Silk Ribbon 2 mm 13 *(yellow)*

Field Flower
Colonial Knot Centre

Silk Ribbon 4 mm 178 *(purple)*
Silk Ribbon 2 mm 13 *(yellow)*

Leaves

Silk Ribbons 4 mm 171 *(green)*
and 2 mm 56 *(green)*

Daisy
Colonial Knot Centre

Silk Ribbon 4 mm 156 *(cream)*
Silk Ribbon 2 mm 13 *(yellow)*

Colonial Knot Rose

Silk Ribbon, 4 mm 159, 163, 157 *(pinks)*

Bow & Basket

Rajmahal 45 *(gold)*
DMC Cotton 869 *(brown)*

Silk Ribbon Cushion

A classical wreath of flowers can be embroidered onto a simple silk cushion, transforming it from an everyday item to an original and graceful piece.

PROJECT IDEAS

Small Blanket
Hat Box
Covered Basket
Lingerie Bag
Wedding
Album Cover

Silk Ribbon Cushion

Fly Stitch Leaves		DMC Cotton 3012 *(green)* Rajmahal 45 *(gold)*
Extended Pistol Stitch Flower		Rajmahal 374 *(rust)*
Forget-Me-Nots Colonial Knot Centres		Silk Ribbon 2 mm 125 *(blue)* Rajmahal 45 *(gold)*
Rose Buds		Silk Ribbon 4 mm 78 *(rust)* DMC cotton 3012 *(green)*
Leaves Glass Bead at Base		Silk Ribbon 4 mm 171, 56 *(greens)* Mill Hill Petite Bead 40557 *(gold)*
Field Flower Bead Centre		Silk Ribbon 4 mm 135 *(peach)* Mill Hill Petite Bead 40557 *(gold)*
Stem Stitch Roses Bead Centre		Silk Ribbon 4 mm 78 *(rust)* Mill Hill Petite Bead 42018 *(pink)*
Bow		Rajmahal 45 *(gold)*

Silk Ribbon Elephants

Beautify these two elephants in the Indian tradition of elephant decorating by embroidering onto silver-shot raw silk with a ribbon-threaded needle.

PROJECT IDEAS

LARGE ELEPHANT
Satin Nightgown
Tissue Box Cover
Knitwear Pocket

BABY ELEPHANT
Needle Case
Baby's Gown
Photo Frame
Shirt Collar

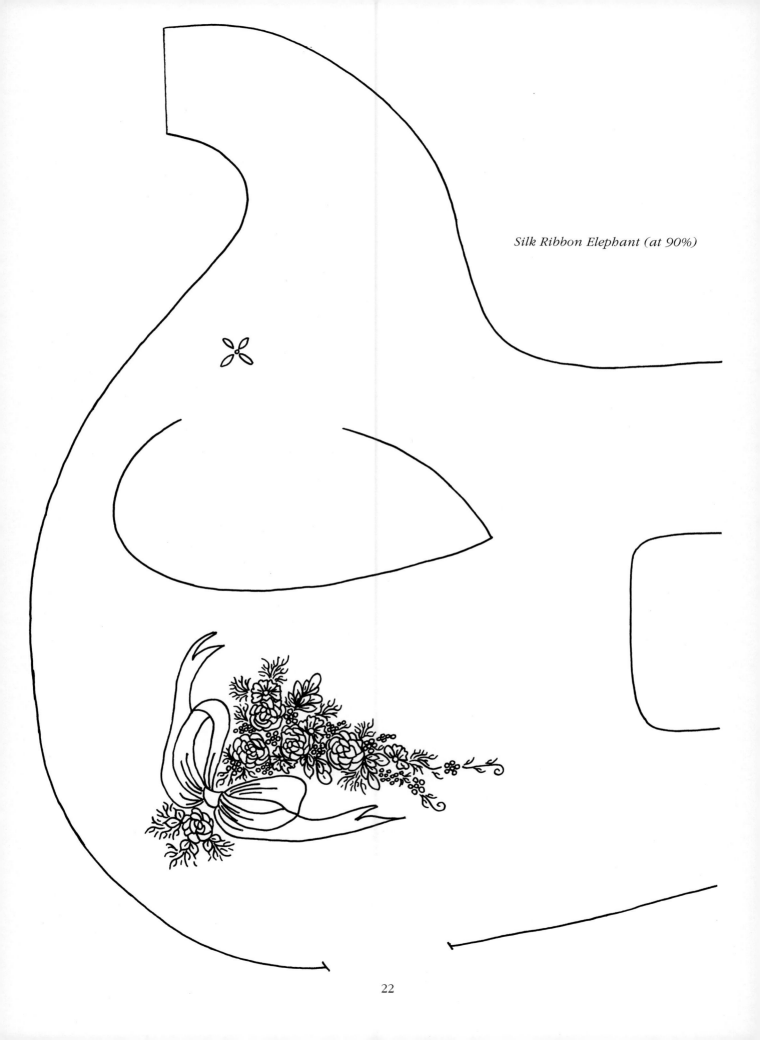

Silk Ribbon Elephant (at 90%)

Fly Stitch Leaves		DMC Cotton 936, 3012 *(greens)*
		Rajmahal 45 *(gold)*
Leaves & Stems		DMC Cotton 936, 3012 *(greens)*
Leaves		Silk Ribbon 4 mm 56 *(green)*
Forget-Me-Nots		Silk Ribbon 2 mm 126 *(blue)*
Bead Centre		Mill Hill Petite Bead 40557 *(gold)*
Colonial Knots		DMC Cotton 223, 224 *(pinks)*
Rose Buds		Silk Ribbon 4 mm 163 *(pink)*
Leaves		Silk Ribbon 4 mm 56 *(green)*
Half Daisy		Silk Ribbon 2 mm 156 *(cream)*
Bead Centre		Mill Hill Petite Bead 40557 *(gold)*
Stem Stitch Rose		Silk Ribbon 4 mm 158, 163 *(pinks)*
Bow		Rajmahal 45 *(gold)*
Ear, Eye & Tail		Rajmahal 226 *(grey)*

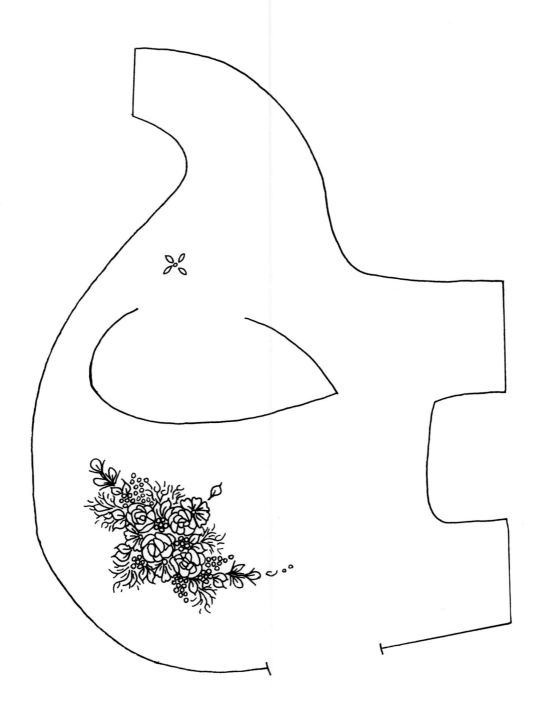

Silk Ribbon Baby Elephant

24

Fly Stitch Leaves		DMC Cotton 936, 3012 *(greens)* Rajmahal 45 *(gold)*
Leaves		Silk Ribbon 4 mm 56, 171 *(greens)*
Rose Buds Fly Stitch Leaves		Silk Ribbon 4 mm 163 *(pink)* DMC Cotton 3012 *(green)*
Forget-Me-Nots Bead Centre		Silk Ribbon 2 mm 126 *(blue)* Mill Hill Petite Bead 40557 *(gold)*
Colonial Knots		DMC Cotton 223, 224 *(pinks)*
Half Daisy Bead Centre		Silk Ribbon 2 mm 156 *(cream)* Mill Hill Petite Bead 40557 *(gold)*
Stem Stitch Rose		Silk Ribbon 2 mm 158, 163 *(pinks)*
Eye, Ear & Tail		Rajmahal 226 *(grey)*

Lavender Bag
& Potpourri Bag

*Good things come in small packages, and these
delicately embroidered silk and organdie
bags prove the truth of the adage
with scented certainty.*

PROJECT IDEAS

LAVENDER BAG
Brooch & Buttons
Teddy Bear Paws
Hankerchief

POTPOURRI BAG
Trinket Pot
Soap Bag

Silk Rabbit

*Let your child drift into a magical world of
fantasy with a gift of this soft rabbit, dressed in a
collar of roses, straight from the pages of
'Alice in Wonderland'.*

PROJECT IDEAS

Hair Clip
Alice Band
Child's Dress
Camisole
Curtain Tie-backs
Jewellery Purse

32

Fly Stitch Leaves		DMC Cotton 3012 *(green)*
Silk Ribbon Leaves		Silk Ribbon 2 mm 171, 156 *(greens)*
Forget-Me-Nots Colonial Knot Centre		Silk Ribbon 2 mm 126 *(blue)* DMC Cotton 422 *(mustard)*
Colonial Knot		DMC Cotton 223, 224 *(pinks)*
Spider Web Stitch Rose		Silk Ribbon 4 mm 158, 163,& 157 *(pinks)*
Stem Stitch Outline		DMC Cotton 422 *(mustard)*

Shoe Fillers

The richness of burgundy and gold, combined with bunches of delicate silk roses embroidered in the softest pink, give these scented shoe fillers a luxuriance reminiscent of the Victorian era.

PROJECT IDEAS

Greetings Card
Blouse Cuffs
& Collar
Handkerchief
Coathanger
Potpourri Sachet
Gloves

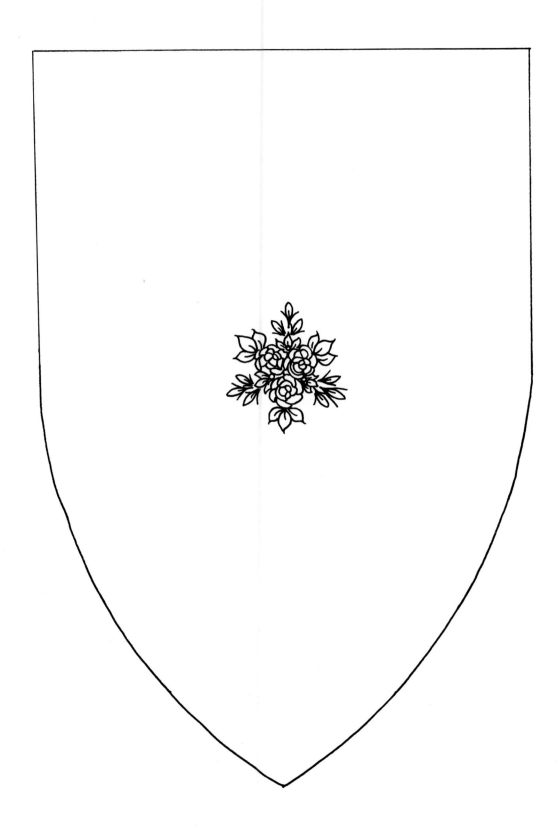

Shoe Fillers

Rose Buds
Fly Stitch Leaves

Silk Ribbon 4 mm 163 *(pink)*
DMC Cotton 3012 *(green)*

Small Ribbon Leaves
Glass Bead at Base

Silk Ribbon 4 mm 171, 56 *(greens)*
Mill Hill Petite Bead 40557 *(gold)*

Stem Stitch Rose

Silk Ribbon 4 mm 163 *(pink)*

Large Leaves

Silk Ribbon 4 mm 171, 56 *(greens)*

Soap Bag

Treat yourself to a little luxury with this organza embroidered soap bag which uses a pretty dough cupid as a central motif.

PROJECT IDEAS

Brooch
Trinket Pot
Baby's Singlet
Handkerchief
Gloves
Slippers

Leaves		DMC Cotton 524 *(green)*
Bullion Roses		DMC Cotton 224, 225 *(pinks)*
Satin Stitch Daisy Colonial Knot Centre		DMC Cotton 453 *(grey)* Rajmahal 45 *(gold)*

Framed Pieces

Embroidery is most often used to embellish personal items. These elegant heirlooms for tomorrow attest to the fact that embroidery can be an art form in itself.

PROJECT IDEAS

Album Cover
Valentine's Pillow
Handkerchief
Box Lid
Hand Mirror
Cushion Cover

Silk Ribbon Heart Arrow Fairy at 80%

Fly Stitch Leaves		DMC Cotton 3013, 3052 *(greens)*
Rose Buds Fly Stitch Leaves		Silk Ribbon 178 *(purple)* DMC Cotton 3052 *(green)*
Wild Rose Leaves		Rajmahal 241 *(pink)* Silk Ribbon 2 mm 56 *(green)* DMC Cotton 3052 *(green)*
Leaves		Silk Ribbon 4 mm 171, 56 *(greens)*
Leaves Stem		Silk Ribbon 4 mm 171 *(green)* DMC Cotton 3013 *(green)*
Chain Stitch Braided Heart		Rajmahal 45 *(gold)* & 241 *(pink)*
Satin Stitch Bow Stem Stitch Outline		Rajmahal 45 *(gold)* & 241 *(pink)*

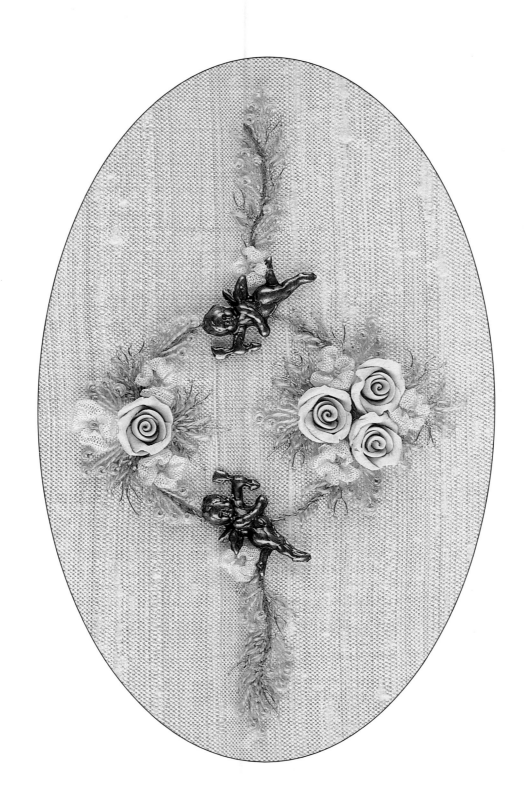

Dough Rose Picture

Extended Pistol Stitch Leaves DMC Cotton 3012, 3013 *(green)*
& 950 *(peach)*
Rajmahal 45 *(gold)*

Field Flower Silk Ribbon 4 mm 156 *(cream)*

Dough Rose
or Bullion Rose DMC Cotton 950 *(peach)*
& 758 *(peach)*

Bronze Cupids

Silk Ribbon Field Flower Bead Centre		Silk Ribbon 4 mm 156 *(cream)* Mill Hill Petite Bead 40557 *(gold)*
Extended Pistol Stitch		DMC Cotton 950 *(peach)*
Silk Ribbon Leaves Fly Stitch Leaves		Silk Ribbon 2 mm 56 *(green)* DMC Cotton 3012, 3013 *(greens)* Rajmahal 45 *(gold)*
Stem Stitch Rose		Silk Ribbon 4 mm 135 *(peach)*

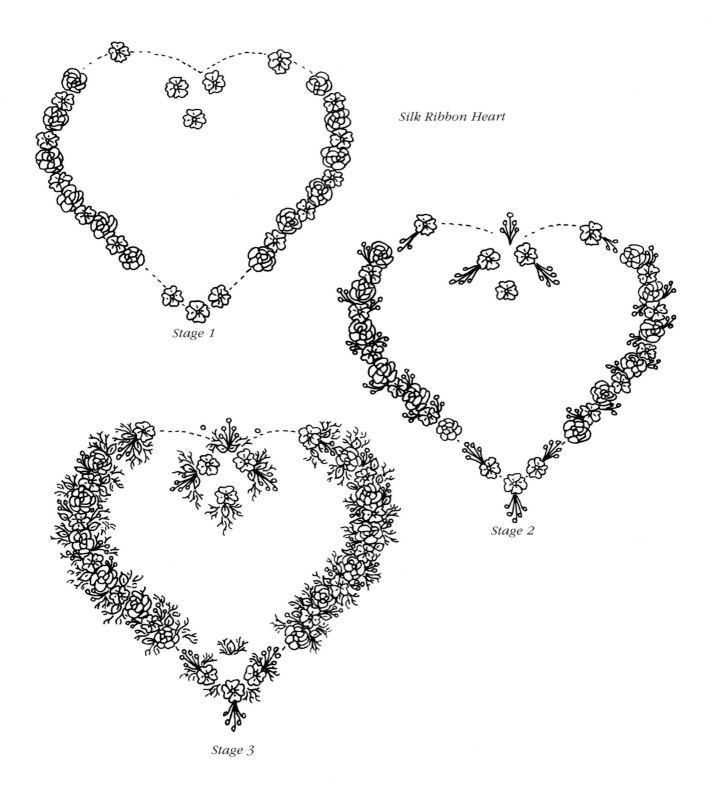

Silk Ribbon Heart

Stage 1

Stage 2

Stage 3

Dough Fairy Garland

Extended Pistol Stitch		Medicis 8223 *(pink)*
Spider Web Rose		Medicis 8314 *(yellow)*
Colonial Knots		Medicis 8328 *(pale yellow)*
Bullion Field Flower Bead Centre		Medicis 8122 *(deep mauve)* Mill Hill Bead 03030 *(antique glass)*

Straight Stitch Daisy Colonial Knot Centre		Medicis, 8381 *(grey)*, Ecru & 8818 *(pink)* Rajmahal 45 *(gold)*
Bullion Rose Buds Fly Stitch Leaves		Medicis 8223, 8224 *(pinks)* Medicis 8405 *(green)*
Bullion Roses Bead Centre		Medicis 8223, 8224, 8225 *(pinks)* Mill Hill Petite Bead 40557 *(gold)*
Fly Stitch Leaves		Medicis 8871, 8407 *(greens)* Rajmahal 45 *(gold)*
Bow		Rajmahal 45 *(gold)*

Rose Fairy

Ribbon Rose Buds Fly Stitch Leaves		Silk Ribbon 4 mm 163 *(pink)* DMC Cotton 523 *(green)*
Colonial Knot Rose		Silk Ribbon 4 mm 158, 163, 157 *(pinks)*
Ribbon Leaves		Silk Ribbon 4 mm 32, 31 *(greens)*
Colonial Knot Wild Rose Leaves & Stems		Rajmahal 742 *(pink)* Silk Ribbon 2 mm 33 *(green)* DMC Cotton 3052, 523 *(greens)*
Satin Stitch Bow		Rajmahal 45 (gold)

Summer Garland & Amy's Hat

A cluster of woven stitch flowers adorn the brim of
Amy's hat, while a captivating garland of summer flowers
embroidered in a blend of threads, ribbons, beads and
pearls graces the centre of a bed cover. From the simple to
the sumptuous, these two embroidery projects cover a
brilliant spectrum of stitches and threads.

PROJECT IDEAS

SUMMER GARLAND
Blanket
Fire Screen
Pram Cover

AMY'S HAT
Knitwear
Mittens
Tea Cosy

Summer Garland at 60%

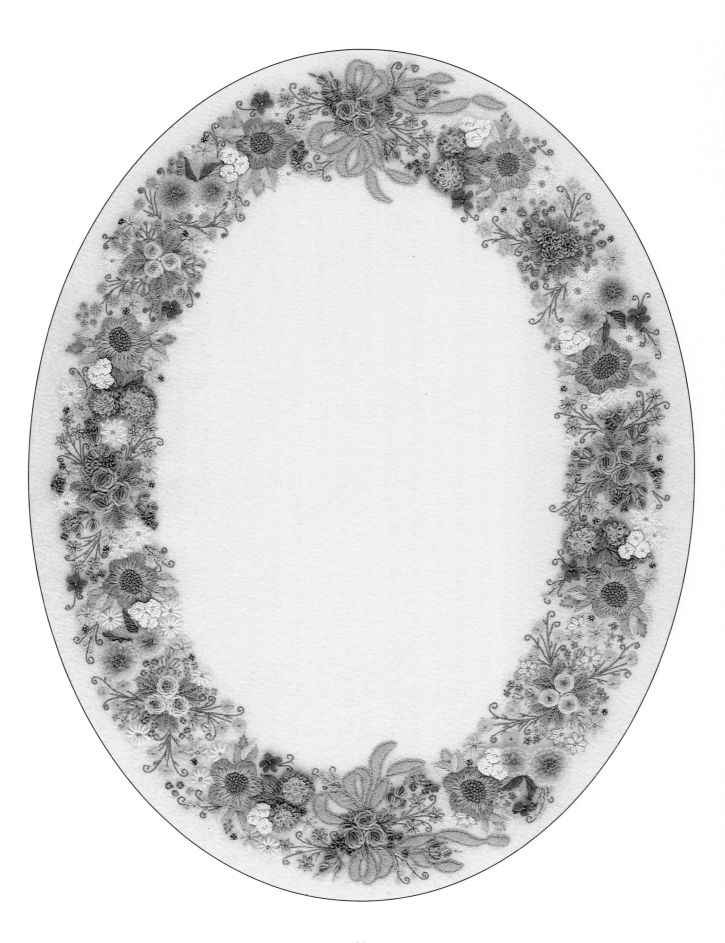

Bead Forget-Me-Not		Beads *(blue & gold)*
Satin Stitch Forget-Me-Not Colonial Knot Centre		Medicis 8211, 8508 *(blues)* Medicis 8314 *(yellow)*
Bullion Stitch Forget-Me-Not Colonial Knot Centre		Medicis 8211, 8508 *(blues)* Medicis 8314 *(yellow)*
Bullion Forget-Me-Not Colonial Knot Centre		Medicis 8211, 8508 *(blues)* Medicis 8314 *(yellow)*
Colonial Knot Forget-Me-Not Colonial Knot Centre		Medicis 8211, 8508 *(blues)* Medicis 8314 *(yellow)*
Straight Stitch Forget-Me-Not Colonial Knot Centre		Medicis 8211, 8508 *(blues)* Medicis 8314 *(yellow)*
Extended Pistol Stitch Flower		Medicis 8119 *(dusty pink)* & 8224 *(pink)*
Bullion Stitch Rose Bud Fly Stitch Leaves		Medicis 8113, 8111 *(pinks)* Split DMC Tapestry Wool 7361 *(green)*
Bullion Rose Bud Fly Stitch Leaves		Split DMC Tapestry Wool 7223, 7221 & 7200 *(pinks)* Split DMC Tapestry Wool 7331 *(green)*
Satin Stitch Rose Buds Fly Stitch Leaves		Split DMC Tapestry Wool 7195, 7193, & 7192 *(apricots)* Split DMC Tapestry Wool 7493 *(mustard)*
Buttonhole Stitch Daisy Bead Centre		Split DMC Tapestry Wool 7579 *(yellow)* Mill Hill Bead 2011 *(gold)*

Daisy-Fly Stitch Tops
(Straight Stitch between Petals)
Bead Centre

Split DMC Tapestry Wool Ecru
Medicis 8223 *(pink)* & 8420 *(green)*
Mill Hill Bead 2011 *(gold)*

Bullion Daisy
Bead Centre

Split DMC Tapestry Wool Ecru
Mill Hill Bead 2011 *(gold)*

Bullion Stitch Tipped Daisy
Bead Centre

Split DMC Tapestry Wool Ecru
Mill Hill Bead 2011 *(gold)*

Lazy Daisy
Bead Centre

Split DMC Tapestry Wool Ecru
Mill Hill Bead 2011 *(gold)*

Shasta Daisy
Bead Centre

Split DMC Tapestry Wool Ecru
Mill Hill Petite Bead 40557 *(gold)*

Woven Stitch Flower
Bead Centre
Stems

Medicis 8223 *(pink)*
Mill Hill Bead 2005 *(pink)*
Medicis 8405 *(green)*

Bullion Stitch Flower
Bead Centre
Stems

Medicis 8818 *(pink)*
Mill Hill Bead 00161 *(crystal)*
Medicis 8405 *(green)*

Bullion Roses

Fly Stitch Leaves

Pearl in Centre

Split DMC Tapestry Wool 7223,
7221, 7200 *(pinks)*
Split DMC Tapestry Wool 7321,
7331 *(greens)*

Stem Stitch Roses

Fly Stitch Leaves

Pearl in Centre

Split DMC Tapestry Wool 7195, 7193,
& 7192 *(apricots)*
Split DMC Tapestry Wool 7493 *(mustard)*
& 7361 *(green)*

Bullion Stitch Roses

Fly Stitch Leaves

Pearl in Centre

Medicis 8113, 8111 *(apricots)*
& 8224 *(pink)*
Split DMC Tapestry Wool 7493 *(mustard)*
& 7361 *(green)*

Spiderweb Stitch Roses

Fly Stitch Leaves

Pearl in Centre

Split DMC Tapestry Wool 7195, 7193,
7192 *(apricots)*
Split DMC Tapestry Wool 7493 *(mustard)*,
& 7361 *(green)*

Wool Roses

Fly Stitch Leaves

Pearl in Centre

Split DMC Tapestry Wool 7195, 7193,
7192 *(apricots)*
Split DMC Tapestry Wool 7493 *(mustard)*
& 7361 *(green)*

Pekinese Stitch Flower

Satin Stitch Leaves

Split DMC Tapestry Wool 7195, 7193, 7192
(apricots) & 7223, 7221, 7200 *(pinks)*
Split DMC Tapestry Wool 7321,
7331 *(greens)*

Satin Stitch Flowers

Colonial Knot Centre

Satin Stitch Leaves

Split DMC Tapestry Wool 7193,
7192 *(apricots)*
Split DMC Tapestry Wool 7221,
7200 *(pinks)*
Split DMC Tapestry Wool 7493 *(mustard)*
& 7422, 7420 *(greens)*

Tubular Knitting Ribbon Rose
Pearl in Centre

Tubular Knitting Ribbon *(soft apricot)*

Bullion Flower
(Daisy Stitch around Bullion)
Stem Stitch Stems
Bead Centre

Medicis 8225, 8119 *(pinks)*

Medicis 8405 *(green)*
Mill Hill Petite Bead 42018 *(pink)*

Whipped Spider Web Flower
Stem Stitch Stems

Medicis 8111 *(soft apricot)*
Medicis 8405 *(green)*

Buttonhole Stitch Flower
Stem Stitch Stems

Medicis 8111 *(soft apricot)*
Medicis 8405 *(green)*

Reverse Buttonhole Flower
Stem Stitch Stems

Medicis 8111 *(soft apricot)*
Medicis 8405 *(green)*

Pistol Stitch Flower
Stem Stitch Stems

Medicis 8111 *(soft apricot)*
Medicis 8405 *(green)*

Stem Stitch Bow

Medicis 8211 *(blue)*

Amy's Hat

Woven Stitch Daisy

Pearl Centre

DMC Tapestry Wool 7722 *(purple)*,
7200 *(pink)* & 7579 *(yellow)*

Woven Stitch Leaves

DMC Tapestry Wool 7331 *(green)*

Teddy Bears

It's fun to dress up in your Sunday best, complete with roses, ribbons and lace, when you are invited to the Teddy Bears' house for tea and cakes in the afternoon.

PROJECT IDEAS

COTTAGE GARDEN
TEDDY
Knitwear Pocket
Book Bag
Guest Towel

SMALL TEDDY
Address Book
Cover
Valentine's Card

Colonial Knots Fly Stitch		Medicis 8103 *(red)* Medicis 8405 *(green)*
Forget-Me-Nots Colonial Knot Centre		Medicis 8331 *(blue)* Medicis 8314 *(yellow)*
Violets Colonial Knot Centre Leaves & Stem		Medicis 8896 *(violet)* Medicis 8314 *(yellow)* Medicis 8407 *(green)*
Colonial Knot Roses Leaves Tree Trunk		Medicis 8223, 8224 *(pinks)* Medicis 8407, 8405 *(greens)* Medicis 8839 *(brown)*
Daffodil Leaves & Stem		Medicis 8328, 8314 *(yellows)* Medicis 8407, 8405 *(greens)*
Blue Bell Stem		Medicis 8211 *(blue)* Medicis 8405 *(green)*
Hollyhock Colonial Knot Centre Leaves		Medicis 8119 *(pink)* Medicis 8314 *(yellow)* Medicis 8405 *(green)*
Shasta Daisy Colonial Knot Centre		Medicis Ecru Medicis 8314 *(yellow)*
Spider Web Stitch Snail Stem Stitch Snail Trail		Medicis 8839 *(brown)* Silver Metallic Thread
Satin Stitch Bee		DMC Cotton Black & 833 *(mustard)*
Bullion Stitch Butterfly Woven Stitch Wings		Gold Metallic Thread

Cottage Garden Teddy at 70%

Lingerie Bag

*The pretty garland of softly coloured flowers
adds a touch of elegance to this
woollen lingerie bag.*

PROJECT IDEAS

Baby's Blanket
Covered Box Lid
Cushion
Pyjama Sack
Hot Water-Bottle
Cover

Lingerie Bag

Stem Stitch Rose Split DMC Tapestry Wool 7221 *(pink)*

Straight Stitch Daisy Split DMC Tapestry Wool 7715 *(blue)*, 7500 *(cream)* & 7200 *(pink)*

Colonial Knot Centre Split DMC Tapestry Wool 7579 *(yellow)*

Bullion Stitch Bud Split DMC Tapestry Wool 7722 *(lavender)*
Lazy Daisy Leaves Split DMC Tapestry Wool 7331 *(green)*

Straight Stitch Split DMC Tapestry Wool 7493 *(mustard)*
Colonial Knot Flower & 7579 *(yellow)*

Leaves Split DMC Tapestry Wool 7321 *(green)*

Straight Stitch Buds Split DMC Tapestry Wool 7221, 7200 *(pinks)*, 7493 *(mustard)*, & 7579 *(yellow)*

Leaves Split DMC Tapestry Wool 7321 *(green)*

Colonial Knot Flower Split DMC Tapestry Wool 7500 *(cream)* 7321 *(green)* & 7722 *(lavender)*

Leaves Split DMC Tapestry Wool 7331 *(green)*

Hat Pin Cushion
& Black Velvet Box

The rose and the daisy, symbols of love and friendship, are here set against black velvet to highlight the delicacy of these embroidered pieces, both of which make elegant gifts.

PROJECT IDEAS

HAT PIN CUSHION
Tea Cosy
Covered Basket
Small Cushion

BLACK VELVET BOX
Evening Bag
Pill Box
Potpourri Sachet

Hat Pin Cushion

Satin Stitch Forget-Me-Not Colonial Knot Centre		Medicis 8211 *(blue)* Medicis 8314 *(yellow)*
Fly Stitch Leaves		Medicis 8405 *(green)*
Satin Stitch Rose Buds Fly Stitch Leaves		Medicis 8224 *(pink)* Medicis 8405 *(green)*
Bullion Tipped Daisy Colonial Knot Centre		Medicis Ecru Medicis 8314 *(yellow)*
Bullion Rose		Medicis 8223, 8224, 8225 *(pinks)*

Black Velvet Box

Forget-Me-Nots Colonial Knot Centre		Medicis 8331 *(blue)* Medicis 8314 *(yellow)*
Fly Stitch Leaves		Medicis 8405 *(green)*
Bullion Rose Buds Fly Stitch Leaves		Medicis 8223, 8224, 8225 *(pinks)* Medicis 8405 *(green)*
Bullion Rose		Medicis 8223, 8224, 8225 *(pinks)*

Bluebird of Happiness Baby's Blanket

The traditional bluebird theme is a perfect design
for either a girl or a boy. This charming blanket,
suitable for both summer and winter, is worked
in fine Medicis wool on the softest
piece of doctor's flannel.

PROJECT IDEAS

Christening Gown
Cot Canopy
Baby's Wrap
Nappy Bag
Lady's Nightgown

Bluebird of Happiness Baby's Blanket

Leaves  Medicis 8405 *(green)*
Rajmahal 45 *(gold)*

Forget-Me-Nots
Bead Centre

Medicis 8211 *(blue)*
Mill Hill Petite Bead 40557 *(gold)*

Satin Stitch Leaves

Medicis 8420, 8405 *(greens)*

Satin Stitch Roses

Medicis 8223, 8224, 8225 *(pinks)*

Satin Stitch Ribbon & Bows

Medicis 8211 *(blue)*
Rajmahal 45 *(gold)*

Stem Stitch Birds

Medicis 8211 *(blue)*

Covered Basket Garland

Flowers have provided perennial inspiration for embroidery designs, and this charming garland adds the perfect finishing touch to a cane basket in which to keep your embroidery threads.

PROJECT IDEAS

Cloth Hat
Pram Blanket
Round Cushion
Covered
Picture Frame
Hat Box Lid
Foot Stool

Covered Basket Garland

Bullion Stitch Flower
Colonial Knot Centre

Medicis 8223 *(pink)*
Medicis 8314 *(yellow)*

Daisy Stitch Leaves

DMC Tapestry Wools 9392, 7331 *(greens)*

Daisy-Fly Stitch Tops
(Straight Stitch between petals)

DMC Tapestry Wool Ecru
Medicis 8816 *(pink)* & 8871 *(green)*

Satin Stitch Daisy
Colonial Knot Centre

Medicis 8331, 8211 *(blues)*
Medicis 8314 *(yellow)*

Wool Rose

DMC Tapestry Wools 7223, 7221 *(pinks)*

Satin Stitch Leaves

DMC Tapestry Wools 9392, 7331 *(greens)*

Cottage Garden

With its wisteria-covered archway and colourful mass of flowers, this wool embroidery design entices you into a magical haven.

PROJECT IDEAS

Guest Towel
Sofa Headrest
Pillow Case
Framed Piece
Clothes

Cottage Garden

Colonial Knot Flower		Split DMC Tapestry Wools 7204, 7210 *(pinks)*
Fly Stitch Leaves		Medicis 8405 (green)
Forget-Me-Nots		Split DMC Tapestry Wool Ecru, 7722 *(mauve)*
Colonial Knot Centre		Split DMC Tapestry Wool, 7493 *(mustard)*
Spider Web Snail		Medicis 8610 *(brown)*
Stem Stitch Garden Seat		

Buttonhole Stitch Hollyhocks
Stem & Leaves

Split DMC Tapestry Wool 7493 *(mustard)*
Split DMC Tapestry Wool 7331 *(green)*

Bullion Rose

Split DMC Tapestry Wool 7210, 7205,
7204 *(pinks)*

Colonial Knot Hyacinth
Stem

Medicis 8333 *(purple)*, 8122 *(plum)*
Medicis 8412 *(green)*

Fly Stitch Lavender
Stem

Medicis 8896 *(lavender)*
Medicis 8407 *(green)*

Daffodil
Stem & Leaves

Medicis 8314, 8328 *(yellows)*
Medicis 8405 *(green)*

Bullion Stitch Stock
Stem

Medicis 8224, 8225 *(pinks)*
Medicis 8426 *(green)*

Buttonhole Bluebell
Stem

Medicis 8331 *(blue)*
Medicis 8407 *(green)*

Colonial Knot Wisteria

Split DMC Tapestry Wool 7266,
7262 *(mauves)*

Lazy Daisy Leaves

Split DMC Tapestry Wool 7363 *(green)*

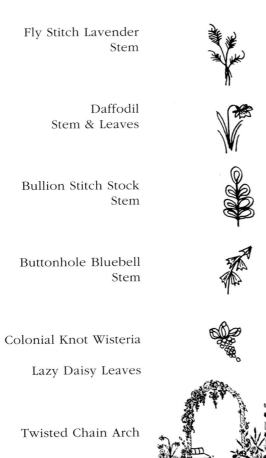

Twisted Chain Arch

Split DMC Tapestry Wool 7845,
7479 *(browns)*

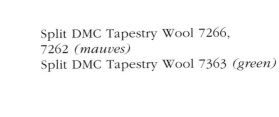

Glossary of Stitches

Threading the Needle with Ribbon

Thread the ribbon through the eye of the needle. Insert the point of the needle back through the centre of the ribbon about 5 mm from the end. Pull the long end of the ribbon taut until the ribbon knots on the needle's eye.

Ribbon Stitch

Bring the needle up through the fabric at point A, spread the ribbon flat on the fabric and return the needle back through the centre of the ribbon at point B. Pull the needle through to the back of the fabric carefully, as the shape of the petal or leaf will depend on the ribbon curling slightly at the tip.

Rose Buds

Using a straight stitch, bring the needle through the fabric at point A and return the needle down at point B. Cover the first straight stitch with a second stitch by starting just below and returning the needle just above the first stitch at point B.

Straight Stitch with Ribbon

Bring the needle up through the fabric at point A. Spread the ribbon flat and return the needle through the fabric at point B.

Colonial Knot Rose

Use three toning shades of silk grading from dark to light. Work a tight group of seven or eight colonial knots in the darkest colour silk to form a centre. Work one row of stem stitch in an anticlockwise direction around the centre knots in the next toning colour. Work a second row of stem stitch in the same manner using the lightest colour.

Field Flower

Work a colonial knot or sew a small bead for the centre of the flower. Using straight stitch, bring the needle up through the fabric close to the centre knot or bead. Keeping the silk ribbon perfectly flat, return the needle back through the fabric, directly behind the first stitch leaving a loop the size of the petal required. Work four or five petals around the centre in this manner.

Stem Stitch Rose

Draw a small circle onto the fabric. Starting on the outside of the circle, work small stitches in stem stitch, sewing in an anticlockwise direction and spiralling inwards until you reach the centre of the flower. Then loop the thread over the centre stitch and return the needle to the back of your work to finish.

Tubular Knitting Rose

Cut 20 cm of tubular knitting ribbon. Thread the needle with a matching colour thread. Pass the needle through the tube of the knitting ribbon, leaving equal lengths of thread at either end of the ribbon. Tie a tight knot with the ends of thread to form a rose. Sew the rose onto your work with the remaining thread. Sew a pearl or bead in the centre of the rose.

Knotting the Thread and Finishing

Thread the needle. Hold the needle near the eye with the thumb and finger of the right hand. With your left hand place the very tip of the tail end of the thread onto the needle and hold in place with the thumb and finger of your right hand. With your left hand, twist the thread around the needle four or five times. Pinch the twists with the thumb and finger of your left hand and with your right hand pull the needle and thread through the twists all the way to the bottom of the thread. You will then have one perfect knot at the end of your thread with which to commence your stitches. On completing each flower or leaf, return the thread to the back of your work. Conceal the knot by inserting the needle and thread through the middle of the knot and tuck it underneath the worked stitches. Weave the needle in and out of the stitches a few times, then anchor off.

Back Stitch

Bring the thread through the fabric and take a small stitch backwards. Bring the needle through again, a little in front of the first stitch, and take another stitch, inserting the needle at the point where it first emerged.

Bullion Stitch

Pick up a back stitch the size of the bullion required. Bring the needle through the fabric at the point where it first emerged but do not pull the needle through. Twist the thread as many times as required to equal the space of the back stitch. Hold the coils between your thumb and forefinger and ease the thread through. Insert the needle back to the starting point to anchor the bullion knot.

Bullion Stitch Flower

Bring the thread through the fabric and take a small backstitch, 2 mm in length *(Diagram 1)*. Leaving the needle in the fabric, twist the thread clockwise around the needle 20 times. Pinch the bullion between your thumb and forefinger and ease the needle through the twists. Pull the thread firmly and secure the bullion by returning the point of the needle back to where it first emerged. Work three more bullion petals in the same manner to form a flower *(Diagrams 2 & 3)*. Work a colonial knot in the centre of the flower.

Buttonhole Stitch

Bring the needle out on the lower (inner) line. Insert the needle on the upper (outer) line, taking a straight downward stitch with the thread below the needle. Pull the stitch up to form a loop and repeat the stitch, working around the circle.

Buttonhole Stitch Daisy

Sew a small bead or work a colonial knot for the centre of the flower. Work seven or eight straight stitches around the centre knot or bead to form a daisy *(Diagram 1)*. Bring the needle up through the fabric at the top of the straight stitch close to the centre bead or knot. Work a buttonhole stitch over the length of each straight stitch *(Diagram 2)*.

Chain Stitch

Bring the needle up through the fabric and hold the thread to the left with the thumb of your left hand. Insert the needle at the point where it last emerged and bring it out again a short distance away. Loop the thread around the needle and pull towards you. Pull through. Repeat the loop by inserting the point of the needle back to exactly where the thread came out at the previous loop.

Daisy Stitch

When commencing the daisy, work from the inside to the outer edge. Bring the needle and thread through the fabric at the base of the petal. Insert the needle back to where it emerged and bring it up again just inside the tip of the petal. Loop the thread around the needle and pull the thread through, anchoring it at the top of the petal with a small stitch. Bring the needle up through the back of your work to start the next petal.

Chain Stitch Braid

Work two parallel rows of chain stitch (Diagram 1). Bring the needle up through the fabric into the centre of the first chain stitch on the left hand side. Pass the needle from right to left through the two chain stitches immediately above, passing over the outer stitches and under the inner stitches (Diagram 2). Continue in this manner until the braid is complete.

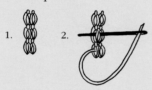

Extended Pistol Stitch

Bring the needle through the fabric. Hold the thread taut and place the needle across the thread, away from the exit point. Wrap the thread around the needle four or five times (Diagram 1). Keep the stalk taut and re-insert the needle into the fabric the length of the stitch required (Diagram 2).

Colonial Knot

Bring the needle up through the fabric at point A. Hold the thread taut with the left hand, away from the fabric. Place the needle under the thread to the right and lift the thread up over the needle from the left to the right, creating a figure of eight. Insert the needle into the fabric close to where it emerged and pull the working thread taut with your left hand so that a firm and tight knot is formed.

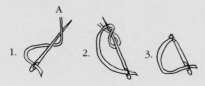

Fly Stitch

Bring the needle up through the fabric to the left of where the stitch is required (Point A, Diagram 1). Take the needle across a little to the right (Point B) and take a small stitch downwards to the centre point (Point C). With the thread below the needle, pull the thread through and insert the needle again below the stitch, at the centre, and anchor in place.

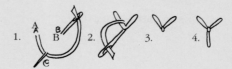

Fly Stitch Leaves

To form the fly stitch leaf, bring the needle up through the fabric at point A. Insert the needle point at B directly above point A and return the needlepoint back to point C, directly below point A *(Diagram 1)*. Keeping the thread below the needle, pull it through and insert the needle again below the stitch to anchor it in place. Continue working downwards from left to right to form a leaf.

Pekinese Stitch

Commence with a row of back stitches. Working from the left, weave through this line of stitches, coming up through one stitch and down through the previous one. Worked in circles, in toning colours, this stitch makes an attractive flower.

Satin Stitch

Work these stitches so that they fit closely together. Care must be taken to keep a smooth and straight outside edge. The stitches may be worked straight or slanted.

Spider Web Stitch

Commence a fly stitch *(Diagram 1)*, then work two straight stitches, one on either side of the fly stitch tail, into the centre of the circle. Weave the thread under and over the spokes, starting at the centre of the circle and weaving until it is filled. Take care not to pick up any of the fabric with your needle *(Diagram 2)*.

Stem Stitch

Work from left to right taking regular, slightly slanted stitches along the line of the design. Always keep the thread below the needle.

Straight Stitch

Bring out the needle at one end and take it down again at the other end.

Twisted Chain

Commence as for ordinary chain stitch, but instead of inserting the needle into the place from where it emerged, insert it into the side of the last loop, taking a good sized slanting stitch and coming out on the line of the design. Pull the thread through.

Whipped Spider Web

Make two crosses, creating eight spokes. Bring the needle up in the centre of the spokes and pull through. Wrap the thread around the spoke just behind the exit thread, slide the needle under that spoke and the next one. Continue to bring the needle back around one and under two spokes until all of the spokes are covered.

Step 1.

Using the darkest colour wool, commence working five satin stitches approximately 10 mm wide from left to right *(Diagram 1)*. Keep the thread above the needle, working downwards and ensuring that the tension is firm but not tight *(Diagram 2)*.

Step 2.

Before commencing this step, change to the lighter toning colour.
Bring the needle up at the mid point of the base of the satin stitches. Take the stitch to the upper right hand corner of the square and return the point of the needle back to the mid point of the base *(Diagram 3)*.

With your right hand, twist the thread clockwise around the needle fifteen times. Pinch the bullion between your thumb and finger and ease the needle through the twists. Pull all of the thread through and lay it down. Pull the thread again, making sure the thread is nice and firm to prevent the bullions from becoming loose and floppy. Anchor off by bringing the point of the needle out into the fabric half a stitch length away. Take a back stitch by placing the needle down through the fabric, half way along the last bullion worked, and return the needle point back to where it first emerged *(Diagram 4)*.

Continue to work around the rose in this manner until the rose is complete *(Diagrams 5 & 6)*. The number of bullions will vary, but five of six is usual.

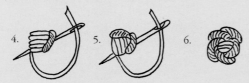

Step 1.

Place a T-pin or needle into the fabric. The distance between where the T-pin enters at point A and emerges from the fabric at point B will determine the size of the petal *(Diagram 1)*.

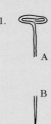

Step 2.

Thread the needle and knot the end. Bring the needle up through the fabric at point B on the left hand side of the T-pin. Wrap the thread clockwise around the T-pin to form three stitches, two on the left hand side of the pin and one on the right *(Diagram 2)*.

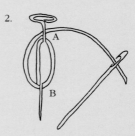

Step 3.

Place the needle under the stitch on the right hand side of the pin *(Diagram 3)*, ensuring that you do not pick up the fabric. Bring the needle through and pull the thread upwards, anchoring in position at the top of the thread ready to commence weaving *(Diagram 4)*.

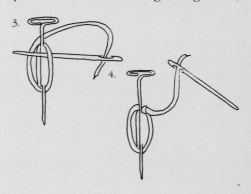

Step 4.
Return the needle under the thread on the right hand side of the T-pin, over the centre stitch and under the next stitch *(Diagram 5)*, and pull the thread through.

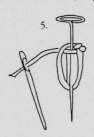

Step 5.
Bring the needle over the thread on the left hand side, under the centre thread and over the right hand stitch *(Diagram 6)*.

Step 6.
Continue weaving in this manner *(Steps 4 & 5)*, working from the top to the bottom until the petal is tightly packed *(Diagram 7)*. Finish the weaving on the left hand side of the petal.

Step 7.
Remove the T-pin from the fabric. Bring the needle up through the loop at the bottom of the petal *(Diagram 8)*, and anchor the stitch by returning the needle to the back of the

fabric at the base of the petal and finishing off. Lift the petal away from the fabric so that it stands slightly clear of the fabric.

Step 8.
Continue constructing the remaining petals by placing the T-pin at an angle of sixty degrees to the first petal and returning to point B at the base of the first petal *(Diagram 9)*.

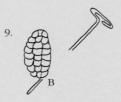

Step 9.
Continue working in this manner until the flower is completed *(Diagram 10)*. Fill the centres with pearls, beads or colonial knots.